Your Customer Service *Selfie*

Your Customer Service *Selfie*

How to Manage Excellent Customer Service

Diara Kendrich

© 2019 by Diara Kendrich
All rights reserved. No part of this document may be reproduced or transmitted in any form or by any means, electronic, mechanical, photocopying, recording, or otherwise, without prior written permission of the publisher.

Cover Design provided by: Anton Pshinka

Printed in the United States of America
First Edition: January 2019

Kendrich, Diara.
    Your Customer Service Selfie: How to Manage Excellent Customer Service / Diara Kendrich.
    ISBN: 9781795368001

CONTENTS

INTRODUCTION 7

    C in "CUSTOMER" is for Contagious 10

    U in "CUSTOMER" is for Unique 20

    S in "CUSTOMER" is for Self-awareness 27

    T in "CUSTOMER" is for Tangible 37

    O in "CUSTOMER" is for Optimistic 42

    M in "CUSTOMER" is for Memorable 51

    E in "CUSTOMER" is for Emotions 60

    R in "CUSTOMER" is for Relationships 69

FINAL NOTE 75

INTRODUCTION

What on earth is a CUSTOMER SERVICE SELFIE? Well, as we are inundated with selfies every day rather it's on your phone, someone else's phone, social media or just saved in a place no one sees – a selfie is simply a photo, and it's all about who? YOU. So if you add, customer service to this lovely word you will have an image of you as it relates to your level of customer service. It's just as simple as that. As we know, when we take a selfie we can be very critical of ourselves and end up with multiples of the same picture. Same pose, same lighting, and the same person. But there's always that one selfie that finally gets the green light, and it's ready to be shared with the world. Why? Because you love it! And why wouldn't you like it, it is your best "you" right?

So now that you've had a "Selfie Refresher 101" let's talk a little bit about why this book is for you or anyone you know that loves customer service. You might say, I don't love it and skip to the next page or close this book. But, I am 99% sure that we all love customer service while working in the field or receiving customer service. There is a beauty in this topic because it is ongoing, happening every moment of the day and it's evolving. It is impacting our ability to make decisions both big and small, it is everywhere we go (unless you're on a deserted island), and it is an experience that can be good, or not so good. And this experience ties into our emotions which leads back to an essential aspect of our lives, decision-making. This book will break down customer service and speak to its importance, provide great tips and insight on how customer service can be significant and/or not so great and how YOU can self-assess your level of customer service.

Working in customer service can come naturally for some and others it may take a great deal of effort. Either way, you can be great at it no matter what industry or line of work you're in. Retail, airlines, food, and entertainment are many of the hundreds of industries that need employees who are customer-service oriented. Entrepreneurs, doctors, lawyers, accountants and others who are self-entities need to focus on customer service if they want to continue to be successful and have returning business, customers, and clients. So, it sounds like we all need to take a customer service selfie and make sure we are equipped and have the right tools in our kit to ensure we are providing the best customer service possible which equates to the best you.

The new selfie is the customer service selfie, and you can delete the one you have now and take a new one if you need to. Or you can add a filter on the one you have now to mold, shape or develop your current one. You are now on the road to gaining a more in-depth understanding of how you can make a difference in your own life and the lives of others by the gift of giving the best you with customer service that sets yourself apart from all the others.

================== NOTE 1 ==================

C in "Customer" is for Contagious

Are you CONTAGIOUS? Whether you know the answer to that question or not, the answer is "You should be!". When it comes to customer service, emotions are involved, and sometimes they are heavy and other times they are not. If you are the person on the receiving end, you want to be in a position to gravitate towards what the person is saying to you and connect with them on a level where you feel comfortable. When the vibe is positive, you should be able to feel that in your connection with them and the energy should coincide with your emotions. That's part of being contagious. Or let's say you are the person serving a customer, you want them to receive what you are saying and show that they enjoy working with you. Ultimately, you want them to do business again with you, and the feelings should be mutual. And we're keeping in mind that this is contagious in a positive way, as the same level of connection could be true if the experience is negative.

I used to work in the bridal industry as a salesperson selling wedding gowns part-time while in school, and I had to learn to work with hundreds of brides and understand their wants and needs, and you wouldn't believe (or maybe you do) all the different personalities and preferences I had to deal with. On average, I would work with between 5-10 brides either in person or over the phone, and as they would come to shop, my number one goal was to get to know them first. I needed to hear the details around when they were getting married, the theme of the wedding, location and any other pertinent information that would help me paint a picture of what they would want. Although that was important, the most crucial role I played was to make them feel comfortable working with me and to do that I had to set the tone at the onset of the conversation. I made an attempt to greet them with a smile, offer them water, make sure they were comfortable while providing me the information and answer any questions they had before looking at dresses. Yes, it would be easy to jump right in and start looking at dresses as soon as they walked in and connected as we went along, but in customer service, we must have a first impression. And in most cases, the impact you make on someone is in the first few seconds or minutes of the conversation. Once you start connecting and letting your personality shine, you are on to something good.

My brides left happy even when they didn't find a dress because I made it my duty to make sure their time was well spent and made them feel valued while they were there. It was truly amazing to see how many would return either the same day or week (sometimes months) later to do business with me. Why? Because we have to be contagious in customer service. It's not always about having the best product on the market. Yes, that helps tremendously, but people will think twice about how well they connected with you, and their emotions are tied to the person who helped them. And truthfully, the product may seem even more appealing when they are working with someone they trust and have built great rapport.

So my whole point is to be contagious in a positive way. When you're contagious, the emotions can be either positive or negative. Be that person that will have a direct impact on those you work with and make a difference. We have no idea what the other person on the receiving end is going through that day. They may want to show and tell how their day is going, and in other cases, their actions may be somewhat demanding, or they may seem irritable. No matter what the situation is, if you are contagious in a positive way, you are already positioning yourself to make a difference in their experience. Also, being contagious reflects who you are and remember we are taking a customer service selfie and focusing on the traits that support being a better you and having a more positive perspective on serving.

Here are 3 simple ways to be contagious:

1. Are you smiling? - Please say yes! This should be the first step in being contagious because people can hear and see your smile and they love it. Even when they are not smiling, this has proven to be a positive way to take action in building rapport with your customer.

2. Ensure that your intent is genuine. – While your smiling, it is essential to focus on being open, honest and merely genuine with the person you are helping. People can see right through a fake smile. And it will help both you and the customer if it is authentic and real as it generates interest from the customer.

3. Make the experience for the customer worth their while. – Think of your interaction with your customer as your moment to shine, but for their benefit. The time with your customer may last for

seconds, minutes, hours, days, months and the list can go on. It depends on what industry you're in and the nature of your business. Either way, focus on making a lasting impression for them and think of customer retention. Your desire should be for them to come back and if you're genuinely contagious, they will want to go back to you.

Self-Reflection Tip:

Think of who you are as a person to your family and friends or when you interact with someone of interest. All of the things you do to create a positive experience for the people in your life should be a representation of how you treat your customers. High level of enthusiasm, showing interest from the beginning to the end of the conversation and demonstrating care and concern are all actions that help you work well with your customers. Be contagious for your customers and know that as a result, it helps you have an excellent overall experience, and you'll want to do it the same way again. The benefit of being contagious in a positive light is for the customer and for you. You will feel as if you've won with the customer and it is proven that anytime we make others feel good, we, in turn, feel good or better than we did before the experience. Take that as a critical point and remember that it is indeed a win-win situation.

ROLE PLAY SCENARIO:

You: *"Hello Mr. Smith, how may I be of service to you today?"*

Customer: *"Well, I'm trying to look for a gift for my wife's birthday, and I would like it to be memorable for her since it is a milestone birthday."*

You: *"Mr. Smith, it will be my pleasure to help you find a wonderful gift for your wife today. Have you thought about getting it personalized?"*

Customer: *"No, I didn't think about that but sounds like a great idea!"*

You: *"Ok, so let's started. Now here's what I'll do, I will help you find a gift your wife will enjoy and can put to good use. We'll find one that has space on it for you to have her name or a sweet message placed on it, which she'll love. Now once we see the gift, I will refer you to one of our close contacts close by that will do the engraving, and you'll receive an excellent discount. I did this for my wife on a milestone birthday, and she still talks about the gift and uses it to this day. Will this work for you?"*

Customer: *"Absolutely! Thanks for making this easy as I was a little anxious about finding the right gift. I really appreciate you helping me."*

You: *"Again, it's my pleasure! You know it's true when they say "A happy wife equals a happy life!"."*

Customer: *(Laughs) "You are absolutely right! Let's go find this gift!"*

Key Points: The words such as "my pleasure" and "I will help you find" are those that immediately lets the customer know you are trying to help. Adding a personal touch or comment to the customer helps you relate better to them. Giving them options and telling them what you can do for them even if you are unable to provide them with all they may need, is essential. Most importantly, part of being contagious is the connection you make by using welcoming words and phrases to reel the customer in. And leaving them with an idea or solution that creates a good memory of their experience working with you. Those particular words can be used in any industry or line of work you are in. Being contagious in a positive way can come in many forms, but this short example should be a starting point to understanding the power in words alone.

Self-Reflection Question

What does being contagious in customer service mean to you?

How will you apply this concept to your line of work?

_____
_____
_____
_____
_____
_____
_____
_____
_____
_____
_____
_____
_____
_____

================== NOTE 2 ==================

U in "Customer" is for Unique

Being unique is extremely important when identifying ways that you can contribute to providing excellent customer service. The first part in realizing how you can be unique is being yourself. No other person on this planet is exactly like you. And if there are any other planets that people live on, guess what? You're still the only you. So the goal here is to be the best you and to do that, you must first identify the characteristics you possess that helps you interact well with others. Is it your bubbly personality? Or if you aren't bubbly, do you have a calming tone that draws people to you? Or if you're more on the serious side, do you demonstrate a level of expertise in everything you do that makes people want to hear what you have to say? Even when you are not entirely proficient in that subject matter? Perhaps there are experiences that you have, and you're willing to share with your customers/clients that helps them feel comfortable working with you. Whatever it may be, everyone has at least one unique thing about them that can take their level of customer service to another level.

Some may know right off the bat what makes them unique rather it is from self-observation or feedback received from others. And there are others who may have to think about what that one thing or several things are that makes them unique. Either way, it's a selfie check to clearly point out and apply those behaviors and characteristics that will make your experience of serving others enjoyable and receptive on the other end. There is nothing like a customer or a client giving you return business and spreading the word amongst their families, friends and social media community how you have made a difference in their lives. In cases like this when a positive word gets spread around, you may not always hear about a specific product or service that was offered. You may just hear about how well they were treated or how someone made them feel. This could be their doctor, accountant, store clerk, phone representative at a company, gym instructor, and the list goes on. This is a perfect example of why customer service is all around us. And the element that makes customer service epic is the unique experience that comes out of it. The uniqueness comes from people identifying what makes people consistently happy and repeating those behaviors. Which in turn, elevates the customers level of satisfaction from what could have been transactional to transformational.

Unique traits consist of a person's thoughts, beliefs, experiences, personality, communication style, level of intelligence, creativity, and much more. All of which makes it even easier to help you pull out those characteristics that you're comfortable with applying to your daily interactions with people. If you find it to be challenging, many personality tests allow you to put your work hat on and use real-life scenarios. These tests help analyze your personality traits and how you would handle situations ranging from easy to the most challenging while working with people.

Below you will see a few ways you can focus on being unique in customer service.

1.   Find out how you are unique - Identify one or two traits that make you unique and would benefit in providing excellent customer service. If you don't already apply these traits, try doing so for at least 21 days (how long it takes to create a habit) and see if it makes a difference in how you feel while helping others and see how customers are reacting to you.

2.   Ask those you trust what they see in you   - Always be ready to ask for feedback and willing to receive it well. Depending on who you ask, the response may be what you expected, and others may identify traits in you that you didn't see or

have never heard anyone say. It could be someone in your family, a spouse or significant other, a good friend or coworker. In some cases, it may be a customer that gives you a compliment and outlines some traits you have that was enlightening to them. Sometimes when you see a pattern in what people are saying about you, this may be an opportunity to take the feedback and run with it – because it's working!

3. Don't be afraid to be unique and think/act outside of the box – If you discover you have a trait that your customers and those around you love, don't be afraid to continue using those traits intentionally. If people like it, why change it right? Or if you self-identify a quality that makes you unique and have not displayed this yet publicly but believe it would have a positive impact on your customers, don't be afraid to demonstrate those in your interactions. You may not know how you are helping others learn more about themselves as you

are giving them some of the great things you have to offer. Be the difference!

Self-Reflection Question

List 3 things that make you unique and how you can implement those traits/behaviors in your interactions with others:

_____
_____
_____
_____
_____
_____
_____
_____
_____
_____
_____
_____
_____
_____

================= NOTE 3 =================

S in "Customer" is for Self-Awareness

Let's take a moment to talk about why focusing on yourself is essential. If you are the one giving customer service and the expectation is to be great at what you do to make a positive impact on others, then it is even more important to be the best you while doing so. I want to take this moment and focus on emotional self-awareness. If you are not feeling 100% when you wake up in the morning, I encourage you to find a way to be in the best position you can mentally and emotionally to better serve others. Our emotions can affect our interactions with others, and positively or negatively impact their emotional state. For example, if you start the day upset and have difficulty letting the anger go before your first few interactions with someone, the experience could go completely wrong. You may not intend for it to go that way because in your mind you are telling yourself to be reasonable and nice, but your emotional state gives off a vibe that others can pick up right away. I, personally have had days where I put the smile on after leaving the house a little upset and spoke to the first person I encountered and asked them how they are doing. Shortly after answering my question, they asked "Are you okay today? You don't seem like yourself". All I could think of was, "How on earth did they know something was wrong with me!?" or "Are they psychic?". The answer is, they can detect something is wrong either by body language, facial expressions, the tone of voice, or they can notice a difference in your demeanor.

Did you know that you can experience a variety of emotions at one time? Or that your feelings can change from one moment to the next? This can happen in one interaction with someone, so it's important to understand the importance of learning how to be conscious of your emotional state. This can be challenging at times, especially when you may be going through various issues in your personal life, work or a combination of both. Stressful situations tend to put us in an undesirable emotional state, and although we try our best to focus on the task at hand, it can take additional effort on our part to manage our emotions. Battling emotions such as anger, sadness, grief, anxiety, and worry may take more than your own efforts to resolve as there may be others that can help (family, friends, trusted coworker, counselor, etc.) The first step to managing them is self-awareness and identifying the necessary steps you may need to take to overcome those emotions and take care of the root issue that's bringing those about. Truth is, we ALL have days where we feel our feelings can overtake us, but it's all about how we manage them.

Taking care of you should be incorporated into your lifestyle even when it gets busy. We can all get too busy where we don't fit time in our day to make that happen, but because it's essential that we do so, we must simply just do it! All it takes is a little time each day, this could be minutes or hours, but every little bit counts. Sometimes we have others around to give us the boost we need to start our day off right, but in some cases, we may only have ourselves. And guess what? That is perfectly fine if we use our time wisely and make it a goal to get our emotions under control before serving others. Giving the best customer service can, in turn, help your emotional state, so it's a win-win for you and the customer.

Here are 5 ways to develop and focus on emotional self-awareness:

1. Daily meditation – Meditation can be helpful as it allows you to go into a space that's calm, uninterrupted and a relaxed state of mind. This helps clear your thoughts and emotions absent of all the distractions that we usually get throughout the day. This may take a few minutes or hours, but realistically you may only have 5-10 minutes, and

that will work. Get your mind clear before you start your day.

2. Journaling – In our busy lives, we may find our days too filled up to start journaling as it sounds like another mundane task to add each day or week, but it would be helpful with self-identifying the emotions you are experiencing each day. When you write those emotions down and tie it back to an experience, you can quickly start to piece together how you can best manage those emotions. If you find yourself happy on most days, a journal can help keep track of those activities or life events that triggered those positive emotions. In contrast, you may become more self-aware of those issues or situations that stir up negative emotions. Self-awareness will eventually help you and a journal is a great tool to have to aid in self-reflection.

3. Seek feedback from a trusted source. – Feedback is a gift is what many say, and this could

serve to be right in any case when we can use it as fuel to become more self-aware. This person could be a family member, friend, coworker, counselor, manager, or even better – a customer! Sometimes we need to hear what others are thinking based on how we treat them and be able to receive the feedback well. Feedback can be constructive, or it can be destructive. However, that will be determined in how we handle it. We need to be open and receptive to the information that is shared with us and accept the things we may or may not want to hear. Feedback is a form of self-awareness, and many have gone from good to great as a result.

4. Self-assessment. – Have you ever taken a personality or self-assessment test? If not, find one online as there are many resources available for free. These tests help you become more aware of your strengths and areas of opportunities. They also help with discovering your values, skills, and abilities. On some tests, it may be appropriate to

put your work hat on while others it may pertain more to your personal life. Either way, you're developing self-awareness, and it can help you identify the areas you may need to focus on to become a better person overall. Or it may help you overcome your emotions, thought processes and behaviors based on individual situations. I have been in a setting with a group of coworkers, and we took a Management By Strengths (MBS) personality test to identify which color group was within our range (Red, Yellow, Blue, Green) and it's incredible how you can all sit around and have an engaging discussion and talk through agreements with the outcome. It helps when you can share the issue with others who know you as they can validate the results. This makes for a healthy discussion that may help with understanding why you do what you do. You can't go wrong with a self-assessment, and once again, it is a form of feedback or self-reflection.

5. Put time aside to do something that makes you better. – Is it spending quality time with your family? Exercising or engaging in a hobby? Are you making it a norm to participate in self-awareness activities? Whatever it may be, the goal is to build up your emotional and mental state, improve your experience in life, and maintain a better work-life balance. If you take care of you first, then you will be in a better position to take care of others. Individuals who do these things find themselves emotionally balanced which makes them a better employer, employee, professional, parent, etc.

Self-awareness gives you a better grasp of the things happening around you and the impact you can have on people and the world. It is to your benefit first, to know what triggers your emotions and be able to manage them throughout your day. Some circumstances are entirely out of our control, and we can start our day off great and boom! Something happens, or we hear news that change how we feel instantly. We must learn to accept the things we cannot change and understand that life happens. And it happens to all of us. It may take time for us to bounce back, but remember the sun always shines after the rain; or in some cases, the storm.

It is important to know that you have what it takes to make the sun shine all around you and for others. Some days it's easy and others it is not. Self-awareness will help you realize your full potential if it is a continual endeavor. Keep this as a focus, and you will only get better and stronger with time.

Self-Reflection Question

What are you doing daily or on a regular basis to help continuously improve your self-awareness? Write down any actions you want to add or remove to help with your focus.

_____
_____
_____
_____
_____
_____
_____
_____
_____
_____
_____
_____
_____

================== NOTE 4 ==================

T in "Customer" is for Tangible

Tangible customer service is an aspect of service that will leave your customer or client feeling valued, appreciated and excited to do business with you. As we know, it is intangible service that initiates their feelings about how you treat them which is being genuine, sincere, understanding, etc. But if you are in the business of serving, think about what it is that you can give to the customer that will make their experience even better. It's compared to the icing on the cake. When a customer has a first-time experience, that may be an opportunity to offer them a special, give them a discount or have them sign up for a loyalty program to earn rewards as they continue to do business with you. Tangible items give customers a reason to come back. However, it must be paired with a good level of customer service which can turn into a great experience.

As a professional in service, it is vital for you to think about tangible items that you may need to improve customer satisfaction. If you or your company can identify the resources necessary to build customer retention, it is truly worth the investment. Once you invest in tangible items for your customers, you will eventually see a return on your investment over time. So what if the budget doesn't allow for multiple sources of tangible items? Don't worry! If you have something to offer your customers rather it's situational, seasonal, or upon request – it doesn't matter much as long as you have something! You can build on those resources over time.

Tangible customer service caters to the senses so it's what the customers can see, hear, smell, feel and taste. Always be thinking about how you can contribute to their feelings when serving them. I absolutely love when I can have an experience that appeals to all my senses, which is relative to how companies are ranked by stars. A five-star hotel will be beautiful outside, and as soon as you walk in, the customer service will be impeccable, the smell is exceptionally refreshing throughout, the beds and linen in the room are super soft, and the food and drinks are fantastic. Now that is a full-on experience that you will not forget and if you could go back, you certainly will!

The other point to mention with being tangible where you can make a tremendous difference is being hands-on with your customers. Any time you can take to spend with the customer and physically show them your product or service and be able to clearly explain the benefits, is worth your time. Customers do business with you for the experience and not just the product or service. The service or product that you're offering could be available to them through other means, but your goal in customer service is to be the reason why they want to come back to you.

Key Point to Remember: It may help to think about what you as an employer, professional, employee, or business owner would need to help create return business. Identify those tangible items or experiences you've had that gave you a reason to give someone a good rating or refer the business/company to others. If you are an employee and your company does not have the tangible item that you think would be beneficial for the customers, don't be afraid to suggest! It may not fit into the budget or be good timing, but who knows if it will eventually be considered. Tangible customer service is all about the person working with the customer and that's YOU. So, keep in mind that even with tangible items, if the interaction is not pleasant the customer can easily be distracted. If you are pleasant and show enthusiasm while providing tangible customer service, once again you are winning. And so is the customer.

Self-Reflection Question

Below, write 3 ways you can focus on reliable customer service and share with someone and make note of their feedback.

1.

2.

3.

Feedback:

_____

_____

_____

_____

_____

_____

_____

_____

_____

_____

================= NOTE 5 =================

O in "Customer" is for Optimistic

Why is optimism good for customer service? It's good because it starts with your attitude and outlook on providing a good outcome for the customer. Too many situations can occur when trying to satisfy a customer that interferes with their ability to be pleased with the final solution. Their expectations may not have been met, an interaction between the customer and employee could go wrong (many of you know what that's all about), a product/service may be questionable with little to no solutions available. If optimism is a goal or an effort of the person providing the customer service, then he/she will work hard towards achieving the ultimate goal, which is meeting the customer's expectations. Our attitude may not always start off in the right place, but it can be redefined and molded into one that most would want to encounter.

Optimism starts in the mind because our thoughts are the beginning point in shaping our words and actions. We must come to a point in our minds in the initial conversation and meeting that we want to create an experience the customer won't forget. A good one. We want them to feel good about the company and/or brand, and it helps to make them feel good about working with you. Have you ever had a customer write or verbally share that they've had a good experience because you or someone you work with did a splendid job helping them? Or have you been that customer to provide this type of valuable feedback based on your interaction with a customer service employee? Well, it's refreshing to know that optimism plays a role somewhere along the line because it is an investment and feedback from the customer is a return on that investment.

Optimism works closely with our "selfie" concept because it is an individual's decision on how they will demonstrate confidence in their role while providing customer service. I'll use another example when I worked in the bridal industry selling wedding gowns. One of my gorgeous and excited customers came in and had a good idea in her imagination what her dream wedding gown would look like. She described it so clearly as if it already existed, which in reality it could if she were to have it custom made. However, we were a store with gowns from many designers both exclusive and non-exclusive she could choose from that would be very similar to what she wanted. I was assigned to assist her for an hour appointment and the first step was to find out what she wanted that would fit her vision and budget. This involved lots of good conversation and rapport building as I began to visualize what she wanted. I informed her how the appointment would go and reassured her that I was there to make sure she found her dream dress in one hour! Now, how did I know I could do that? Optimism. This attitude takes you to a place where you are incredibly confident in your ability to get a goal or task accomplished without allowing barriers and fears to interfere. Of course, there will always be factors that may impact a customer's decision to make a purchase, but I made the decision upfront in every encounter to focus on the positive. I wanted what was best for them because, in the end, I would have a happy customer, a solid sale, repeat business and referrals. A win-win situation for everyone involved should be our goal in every customer service interaction.

Three key things to remember when being optimistic are:

1. Build rapport and connect - We typically have a matter of seconds to initially connect with a person and make a positive impression when we first meet them. If this opportunity is ruined, it could negatively impact the ability to connect and move forward with establishing a positive influence on the customer. Get to know something about them, acknowledge a good thing you may already know

about them, give a compliment, thank them for their business in advance, smile, exude positive energy, and continue to do all the things you can think of to build rapport and connect with your customer.

2. Think positive inside and outside the box - In many cases, the connection formed with a customer entails speaking the obvious and getting straight to the point. Being positive the entire time is essential to make this an enjoyable experience even if the customer knows what outcome to expect. In other cases, it may take your knowledge and expertise to think of ideas and options outside the box to positively encourage the customer and help them gain confidence in the product or service you are offering. It can feel as if you are starting from scratch which makes it even more important to be optimistic, patient and try your best to put them first.

3. Always think about future opportunities - If you've made your customer's day, there's a great chance you had a good day too. It typically feels good to make another person happy and know that you contributed to that happiness. The result of being optimistic is repeat customers, as they will have a desire to repeat the experience you gave them. If you were to go to two different coffee shops and the coffee tasted the same, but one shop gave you a better experience (calming environment, smiling employees, excellent and consistent customer service) then you would choose the one that makes you feel good. It's obvious, but very accurate when determining who to give your business to and which shop you would refer others to. At that point, you are giving a future opportunity to that coffee shop to gain more satisfied and frequent customers who will do the same as you did and spread the word about their great experience. And it all started with the

employees making the decision to treat you well and maintain a positive attitude.

Now as we return to how this applies to a "selfie" mindset, remember that it is up to you to look in the mirror and ask yourself if you are that optimistic person while working with customers. When you make the decision to be this way during every interaction with your customer even when you are not feeling your best, you will have a good outcome. In some work environments, there are incentives around recognizing good customer service, some of which are tangible, and others are verbal. Either way, the incentive may serve as a source of motivation however the desire to put a customer's needs first and do your best to help them should become the driving source to help. If you are working in a customer service environment where incentives and recognition are the norms, that is indeed a healthy place to be. If you are not receiving recognition (verbal or non-verbal), then you may want to suggest to your leader to implement a recognition program. If you are already a leader in customer service, it is vital for you to seek ways you can include recognition for your employees. Again, recognition is not the only driver of motivation, but it can inspire employees to want to go the extra mile for their customers. Life happens to everyone at some point, and there are days where we may not feel like going over the top, but a business or company with good leadership and recognition will breed success with influencing their employees to excel in their role.

Be optimistic about creating an environment that is conducive to giving excellent customer service. Be optimistic about yourself and your individual ability to demonstrate skills that will elevate your customer service. It all begins with you so make sure this selfie has optimism written all over it.

Self-Reflection Question

What are some ways you deal with difficult customers/clients while being optimistic? List how you have overcome any challenges with being optimistic.

_____
_____
_____
_____
_____
_____
_____
_____
_____
_____
_____
_____
_____

================ NOTE 6 ================

M in "Customer" is for Memorable

What do you want people to remember when you are providing customer service? Do you want to meet their need and move on to the next? Or do you want to give them a product/service paired with a memorable experience that makes them want more? I'm hoping your desire is the latter because creating excellent memories for the customer is the key to success in the world of customer service. Every person on this planet including you will enjoy a product or service, even more, when you have countless and consistent good memorable interactions with the business.

Have you ever visited a restaurant or store where the employees took the time to get to know their customer's name? I can speak from experience from my first visit at a local family-owned restaurant close to my workplace. The specialty food was philly sandwiches and chicken wings, and my favorite meal was the steak philly combo with lemon pepper wings. The food is delicious, and even with limited hours, the restaurant stays very busy throughout the day until it closes in the early evening. The best part about my visit (and many others can attest the same) is the gentleman who took the orders and would ask your name up front, and the very next time you visit, he will remember you. And from that point on, you feel welcomed as if you are a part of the family. To see the him treat the other customers the same when I would sit and dine-in was extremely impressive. If you were to read the reviews of the restaurant online, his acknowledgment of customer names is mentioned repeatedly. He passed his communication style down to the other employees, and it became a regular practice for anyone who takes your order. The food they serve is delicious, however there are many other restaurants in the area that have good food. The fact that I feel welcomed every time, there were days that I didn't necessarily have a taste for the philly steak or wings, and I would still go because I wanted to go somewhere that made me feel good. And of course, I wasn't disappointed after I ate my meal. I could always expect a big smile, hear my name several times, receive a check-in at my table to see how everything is going and hear a proper good-bye. This happened every time I went, and that first visit eventually turned into years of me being a loyal customer. And I am still excited to go there today.

The second and probably most important factor in this experience is that I have decided to make sure that I invite others and spread the word about this excellent local restaurant. It brings me joy to talk about how good the food is and transition to the superb customer service aspect. Word of mouth can be the best form of advertisement for businesses, and I'm pretty sure the volume of business increased through referrals. There are no commercials, billboards, signs or other visible advertisements for this restaurant. The same way I found out, from a fellow employee is the same way many others learned of this restaurant.

So I say that to say this, referrals and sharing good experiences will go a long way for you as the one who is providing the customer service. You want to take a look at what you are doing and saying to the people you serve to make them return and want to share their experiences with others. How can you do that? How can you make a lasting impression on someone even if the interaction may only last minutes at a time?

See the tips below:

1. Greeting - The moment you see a customer or hear their voice if it's over the phone for the first time, greet them kindly. It doesn't matter what type of day you've had or if the previous customer wasn't that great; greet every customer with a kind tone and positive words. It makes a huge

difference as you are setting the tone on how the rest of the conversation will flow.

2. Pay close attention - Listen to what they ask you or mention because this is the first indicator of what they need. It is up to you to identify their needs fast and give them a quick response to assure them you are there to help.

3. Answer questions and provide options - The customer is leaning to you for your knowledge and expertise. And if you don't know or have the answer readily available, let them know you will find out how to help. Offer all relevant options that will help enhance their experience and allow them an opportunity to choose. This is imperative because a customer can choose to walk out and not return if they come in with one want/need in mind and no other options are offered. Even if they still don't choose to do business because you may not have what they want or expected, they will

always value your assistance and willingness to give them other options if available.

4. Get personal - The personal touch is an excellent way to create a memorable experience for the customer. Use their name, remind them of a previous experience you had with them, use compliments, and/or acknowledge any events happening in their life (birthday, anniversary, or other celebrations) that they speak of. Talk to them in a tone that is genuine and warm, not robotic and cold. If a customer is happy or sad, it is up to you to manage how you will speak with them in the most inviting and most appropriate tone. Your choice of words will go a long way and getting personal entails using positive words the customer will not forget.

5. Show appreciation - When a customer leaves your presence or hangs up if you're on the phone, are they aware that you appreciate them? The only sure way to know without having to second guess

is to tell them. Every. Single. Time. It is a beautiful feeling to hear a simple "thank you for your business" during or after being provided excellent customer service. This form of appreciation doesn't cost a thing, and it makes a huge impact. Other ways to show appreciation to a customer include special offers, discounts, freebies, etc. The one important thing to remember when appreciating the customer rather it's only verbal or tangible is how you deliver to the customer.

The common denominator in creating a memorable experience for the customer is you. That's your selfie check! Ask yourself if you are up to implementing these suggestions and behaviors into your daily interactions. Consistency in doing so will breed the results you want to ensure you have a desirable experience helping them. It all starts with you and your decision to create that memory, putting yourself in their shoes and having fun with it. Memories can be both good or bad, so the focus should be to turn bad situations into good ones and taking a basic experience to the next level of greatness. You are the impact, and you are their memory. Make it worth everyone's while, including yours.

Self-Reflection Question

Write down the most memorable experience you've had while providing great customer service? What role did you play in creating a good experience for the customer?

_____
_____
_____
_____
_____
_____
_____
_____
_____
_____
_____
_____
_____
_____

================== NOTE 7 ==================

E in "Customer" is for Emotions

Emotions, we all have them and know they can change by the day, hour or minute. They can be impacted directly, indirectly or for an unknown reason. When working with people in the beautiful world of customer service, your emotions may not always be conducive to being upbeat and warm as you want it to be. Which brings me to the point of this segment as we focus on your emotions as the priority. If your feelings are intact first, then you will be able to give your absolute best to your customer. If not, the experience of the customer can be different in a way that they can pick up on the negative emotion and run with it. That's not what we want, so it's imperative to do a selfie check before your first encounter of each day. And it's not a bad idea to do a selfie check first thing in the morning before you leave the house. It's very similar to setting the temperature where you want it to be so for the remainder of the day you stay the same way you set it.

As I've worked in various industries in customer service, I've learned that keeping my emotions in check is the key to enjoying what I do and doing it well. We all have good days, really good days, bad days, and really bad days. What I mean by that is we can wake up feeling just okay, and as the day goes along there may be people or circumstances that make us feel good or bad. The really good and really bad days are those days you wake up feeling excited or down and the day continues the same way you woke up, and other external factors will have no influence on how you feel. What I've learned is that we can choose to feel happy on those days we are not. If it's to a point where I feel overwhelmed and have difficulty feeling happy, I seek some sort of internal and/or external motivation to help. Especially when I know I have to work directly with people that day, and it's not a rainy Saturday when I can have a pity party and hide under the covers all day.

    I recall a day when I was scheduled to work with five different customers by appointment, and I woke up feeling as if I was under a dark cloud before my day even started. I tried to meditate and tell myself I was going to have a wonderful day and put on my favorite song on my drive to work. By the time I got out of the car and walked into the building, I felt a little better, but I still felt down and didn't understand why I couldn't relieve the depressing feeling. The moment I sat down with my first customer and saw how excited they were about the products we had to offer and knowing I had to be the one to help her maintain that excitement, I made the immediate decision to turn on my happy button. The moment I realized it is truly not about me and it's all about serving others and making them happy, I knew I would be able to deliver excellent service even when I'm not feeling my best. The beauty in helping others and choosing to be happy is when the result leaves them in a better place than they were before they worked with you. You've heard the saying "Happy Employees equals Happy Customers." I learned at that moment, this is the truth. As I speak specifically to those difficult times when choosing to be happy is challenging, it is imperative to know that we must put others wants/needs first and seek to make them happy.

In most cases, you will end up happy or at least happier than you were before you helped them. It was interesting that this method helped bring me to a happy place, and not my favorite song and all the other self-motivating things I did before I came to work. What we must understand is that life happens to everyone and the most authentic way of handling draining emotions is accepting it for what it is and take action to change how you feel. Choosing to be happy to help others is another win-win situation where our emotions play a pivotal role in delivering excellent customer service.

As we have stepped into the realm of emotions, let me briefly mention how emotional intelligence is a key concept in customer service. Emotional intelligence is the ability to identify, manage and access emotions within yourself and others. If you can apply emotional intelligence to your customer service style, you would be able to understand the impact of both positive and negative emotions in your daily interactions. Although you may have good days most of the time, your customers may not, and you can run into a situation where you have to identify how to deal with those individuals.

The first step is knowing which path you must take to get a positive outcome. If a customer is sad, do you approach them with an upbeat and high-pitched tone and a super radiant smile the whole time? That may work for someone, but if you tune in to their emotions, you may want to have a more calm and soothing tone to let them know you recognize they are sad. We do not wish to ignore feelings but acknowledge them to the best of our ability and then proceed with the best form of communication that will help make a positive connection with the customer.

Here are 3 tips on incorporating emotional intelligence when working with a customer:

1. Understand how emotional intelligence benefits you - When you get to a point where you are intentionally taking the time to manage your emotions and those of others, this is personal growth. Continue to take advantage of every opportunity to quickly identify the feelings of your customer and then proceed with adopting a style that will create a sense of authenticity. Recognize when they are happy, sad, angry, confused, uncertain and acknowledge the emotion and do your best to turn it into a favorable situation. The customer will connect with you much easier when

you recognize how they feel and come to a resolve and positive outcome.

2. Pay close attention to the signs of emotion - What are the signs? They are words, body language, facial expressions, reactions, the tone of voice, etc. These signs are the tell-all for you to know if the customer is willing to do business with you, enjoying the experience or not and has the desire to return. If these signs are positive, continue to match them with yours and stay positive. If the signs come off negative, it is important to be timely in asking defining questions to help you understand their thoughts and show empathy. And once you're aware, you will do your due diligence to ensure they are well-informed and satisfied in the end.

3. Know what your customers want and how they think - This may come naturally for some, while others may have to do a little research. It's important to understand what makes your

customers develop an interest in your product/service and incorporate that information into your conversations. Your conversation should be informational, intriguing and when possible, you want to surprise customers with something they don't know. Is it the upcoming product that's being offered, a new item coming to the menu, an additional service, a discount/sale next week or month? Put that buzz in your customers' ears as all this new and exciting information creates positive emotions in your customers. This can help turn that negative emotion into a positive one, and for those who were already positive, you can turn them into a raving fan of your company.

These are just a few tips on emotional intelligence that will ultimately help you better manage the emotions of your customers as well as your own. Decisions to purchase products/services are primarily emotional driven, so it is important to know that emotions play a major role in providing exceptional customer service.

Self-Reflection Question

Identify your strengths and areas of opportunity as it relates to how you manage the emotions of yourself and others.

_____
_____
_____
_____
_____
_____
_____
_____
_____
_____
_____
_____
_____

================= NOTE 8 =================

R in "Customer" is for Relationships

What relationship is the most essential in providing excellent customer service? Does it start with your relationship with your customer? Well, we all know that is extremely important, but since we've learned the importance of selfie checks, the most important relationship to have is with yourself. Do you have a host of things you absolutely love about yourself (personality, energy, ability to connect with others, etc.)? Do you have confidence and feel good about being you? Are you willing to consistently learn and work on your personal and professional development? If you've answered yes to all these questions, then you are in the best position to be able to give the top of the line customer service. Why is a relationship with yourself important? Because when you are happy and confident within, it is much easier to serve others genuinely. Even on your worst day, when you truly love yourself, it is less challenging to empathize with others as you have on the inside of you what is needed to meet the needs of others. Learn to love yourself more each day, and people will love you!

Next is the relationship building with the people around you. These are other employees, leaders, partners in business, clients/customers; everyone with whom you are in contact with. As you focus on building positive and lasting relationships, it is imperative to think of the current moment and the future when working with someone. Learn to leave people with a lasting impression as if it's the last time you will have the opportunity to speak with them. It's like telling a spouse/significant other or close family member/friend you love them on that last conversation of the day. Start a habit if you haven't already, thanking the people you work with, after conversing with them. Make them feel good speaking with you, ask questions, provide answers, talk about things they want to hear, get personal with them, share some commonalities, educate them and explain the reasons why their needs can or cannot be met at that time. People like to connect and build a relationship with those they are working closely with and/or giving their business to short or long-term.

Here are 3 tips more in detail on how to build strong and positive relationships:

1. Take advantage of making a lasting impression at your first encounter - When a customer speaks to you, it wouldn't matter if you are the CEO, owner of the company or employee; you must make sure you give them every reason to want to continue doing business with you. Choose your words wisely, smile, answer their questions and use your expertise to serve them. Once they have finished interacting with you, they should be looking forward to the next time and spread the word about their experience.

2. Give your customers an opportunity to provide feedback - In your line of work, you are expected to be the expert however for your business/company to continue to flourish, you need to hear directly from the customers. They need to be able to tell you what they expect or would like to see from you. The customers' feedback will allow you to hear what improvements and changes you need to make, and they can give you ideas on how to innovate your business or strategy. Their feedback is valuable, and when the customer sees their suggestions and comments are making a difference, this will strengthen the relationship.

3. Exceed their expectations and go the extra mile - This behavior should be the norm because it is already an expectation from the customer to receive excellent customer service. However, exceeding them and going out your way to help them is like icing on the cake, with a little cherry on top. Don't hesitate to surprise and delight your customer, give them an extra tip or advice even

when they don't ask for it and make them feel special. When you do these things, the customer will also appreciate the times that you are unable to satisfy their needs or wants at that time. The effort in what you do and how you go about helping others makes the difference in their perception of your willingness to make them feel valued.

Excellent and stable relationships are essential in everything we do, especially in customer service. Negative relationships are toxic, destructive and unhealthy for a person and a business while the positive ones are safe, constructive and healthy. It is up to you to be sure to maintain excellent relationships with yourself and all the others you work with to find enjoyment in what you do every day.

Self-Reflection Question

Reflect on a moment when you were able to build a solid business relationship with someone. What skills and behaviors do you feel are necessary to build good rapport with your customers?

_____

_____

_____

_____

_____

_____

_____

_____

_____

_____

_____

_____

_____

================ FINAL NOTE ================

A customer service selfie is something you know all about at this point. I hope you had an opportunity to review both internal and external factors which contribute to your ability to provide above exceptional service in your field of work. Once again, customer service is everywhere we go and it's important to understand what you need to do and how you can help someone focus on the skills and behaviors needed to enhance a customer's experience. The moment we get into a mindset of serving rather than just doing a job, our behavior changes. And although some information provided to you as a note may seem like common sense, we all know that it's not too common in many places and amongst many people. If it were common, we would all have excellent experiences everywhere we go and that would be lovely. But unfortunately, that is not the case.

It is now time for you to take these customer service notes and apply the ones you feel would work best, which may only be a few or all. This is all about viewing yourself as a person who has what it takes to make a positive impact in any industry you're in, recognizing that customer service doesn't have to be included in your title. It's who you are on the inside and who you can become to influence and enhance the experiences of others. **C**ontagious, **U**nique, **S**elf-Awareness, **T**angible, **O**ptimistic, **M**emorable, **E**motions, **R**elationships are key words that turn into effective behaviors which helps with being the best you. As you develop and perfect your selfie, consider these factors and you can become one of the greatest in serving others and demonstrating excellence in customer service.

ABOUT THE AUTHOR

Diara Kendrich has a background which includes Sales, Management, Consulting, and Customer Service. She holds a Bachelor of Arts in Psychology from Argosy University and earned her Master of Science in Psychology, specializing in Industrial/Organizational Psychology, from Capella University in 2012. Diara is the author of an inspirational book titled, "I live. I struggle. I WIN!" published in 2011 and a business book titled "Who Farted in the Boardroom? – How to Outscore Conflict in the Workplace" published in 2013. In her writing, she has combined her work experience and educational background with her passion in customer service, training and leadership.

www.ingramcontent.com/pod-product-compliance
Lightning Source LLC
Chambersburg PA
CBHW070130240526
45468CB00002BA/770